W9-BPM-997

A PRIMARY SOURCE HISTORY OF THE UNITED STATES

THE NEW REPUBLIC

1763–1815

George E. Stanley

WORLD ALMANAC® LIBRARY

Please visit our web site at: www.worldalmanaclibrary.com
For a free color catalog describing World Almanac® Library's list of high-quality
books and multimedia programs, call 1-800-848-2928 (USA) or 1-800-387-3178
(Canada). World Almanac® Library's fax: (414) 332-3567.

Library of Congress Cataloging-in-Publication Data available upon request from publisher.
Fax (414) 336-0157 for the attention of the Publishing Records Department.

ISBN 0-8368-5825-5 (lib. bdg.)
ISBN 0-8368-5834-4 (softcover)

First published in 2005 by
World Almanac® Library
330 West Olive Street, Suite 100
Milwaukee, WI 53212 USA

Copyright © 2005 by World Almanac® Library.

Produced by Byron Preiss Visual Publications Inc.
Project Editor: Susan Hoe
Designer: Marisa Gentile
World Almanac® Library editor: Alan Wachtel
World Almanac® Library art direction: Tammy West

Picture acknowledgements:
The Granger Collection: Cover (upper and lower left); Library of Congress: Cover (upper and
lower right), pp. 5, 6, 10, 12, 13, 17, 18, 19, 21, 22, 23, 24, 26, 27, 29, 32, 34, 37, 38, 41, 43;
National Archives: pp. 8, 14, 15, 16, 25

All rights reserved. No part of this book may be reproduced, stored in a retrieval system,
or transmitted in any form or by any means, electronic, mechanical, photocopying,
recording, or otherwise, without the prior written permission of the copyright holder.

Printed in the United States of America

1 2 3 4 5 6 7 8 9 09 08 07 06 05

Dr. George E. Stanley is a professor at Cameron University in Lawton, Oklahoma. He has authored
more than eighty books for young readers, many in the field of history and science. Dr. Stanley recently
completed a series of history books on famous Americans, including *Geronimo*, *Andrew Jackson*,
Harry S. Truman, and *Mr. Rogers*.

CONTENTS

Through the examination of authentic historical documents, including charters, diaries, journals, letters, speeches, and other written records, each title in *A Primary Source History of the United States* offers a unique perspective on the events that shaped the United States. In addition to providing important historical information, each document serves as a piece of living history that opens a window into the kinds of thinking and modes of expression that characterized the various epochs of American history.

Note: To facilitate the reading of older documents, the modern-day spelling of certain words is used.

CHAPTER 1

A Cry for Independence

1763–1774

The American Revolution did not happen overnight. It was many years in the making and was influenced by various circumstances. When the French and Indian War ended with the defeat of the French in 1763, the Indian tribes of the Ohio River Valley feared that the British would take their lands, so they attacked British forts from Niagara to Detroit. But in October 1763, they, too, signed a peace treaty with the British. This treaty ceded control of all land west of the Appalachian Mountains to the Indians, which meant the colonists were forbidden to settle the territory that they had won from the French. This move inflamed the colonists.

TAXATION WITHOUT REPRESENTATION

The cost incurred by the French and Indian War put the British government deeply in debt. Prime Minister George Grenville felt that the colonists, who had benefited from the defeat of France, should pay for the war with taxes on foreign imports. The British passed the Sugar Act of 1764, which levied taxes on various imported food items, such as wine,

THE SUGAR ACT: 1764

… For every hundred weight avoirdupois of such foreign coffee … two pounds, nineteen shillings, and nine pence….

For every ton of wine … of the Madeiras … seven pounds….

For and upon every gallon of molasses or syrups [one of the main commodities smuggled into the colonies and the reason for the act's name] … the sum of three pence….

coffee, and sugar. The colonists were angered. Without a voice in Parliament, they considered the Sugar Act to be taxation without representation. Prime Minister Grenville ignored the colonists' dissent, and in 1765, the Stamp Act was passed, requiring all printed material to have a stamp, which was sold by the government. There was a storm of protest. Colonial leaders asked the people to boycott, or stop buying, British goods.

THE STAMP ACT: 1765

... For every skin or piece of vellum or parchment, or sheet or piece of paper, on which shall be ingrossed, written or printed, any declaration ... or other pleading, or any copy thereof ... within the British colonies and plantations in America, a stamp duty of three pence....

For every skin or piece of vellum or parchment, or sheet or piece of paper, on which shall be ingrossed, written or printed, any donation, presentation, collation ... or any writ or instrument for the like purpose, or any register, entry, testimonial, or certificate of any degree taken in any university ... or seminary of learning, within said colonies ... a stamp duty of one shilling....

◄ A protest against the Stamp Act is reflected in this 1766 cartoon entitled "The Funeral of Miss Anne Stamp."

In October 1765, representatives from nine colonies met to demand an end to the tax. They reasoned that as British colonists, they were entitled to the same consideration as their counterparts in England—that no tax could be levied upon them without their consent. To this end, they drafted the Resolutions of the Stamp Act Congress on October 19, 1765.

THE BOSTON MASSACRE

The colonist boycott of British goods had begun to hurt merchants in Great Britain. It was also making King George nervous. He fired Grenville and appointed Charles Townshend as his new prime minister.

When Townshend repealed the Stamp Act, the colonists believed that their boycott had succeeded.

RESOLUTIONS OF THE STAMP ACT CONGRESS: 1765

The members of this Congress ... make the following declarations ... respecting the most essential right and liberties of the colonists, and of the grievances under which they labor, by reason of several late Acts of Parliament....

II. This His Majesty's liege subjects in these colonies, are entitled to all the inherent rights and liberties of his natural born subjects within the kingdom of Great-Britain.

III. That it is ... essential to the freedom of a people ... that no taxes be imposed on them, but with their own consent, given personally, or by their representatives.

▲ This 1770 engraving by Paul Revere depicts the bloody Boston Massacre.

PRESTON'S ACCOUNT OF THE BOSTON MASSACRE: 1770

... On Monday night about eight o'clock, two soldiers were attacked and beat. About 9 some of the guard came to and informed me, the town inhabitants were assembling to attack the troops, and that the bells were ringing as a signal, and not for fire.... The troops rushed thru' the people ... [and] kept them at a distance....

The mob still increased, and were more outrageous, striking bludgeons one against another, and calling out, "Come on, you rascals, you bloody backs, you lobster scoundrels; fire if you dare...." Some well-behaved person asked me if their guns were charged. I replied, yes. If I intended to order the men to fire. I answered no. While I was speaking a soldier having received a severe blow with a stick, instantly fired....

A general attack was then made on the men.... Instantly, three or four of the soldiers fired....

The mob then ran away, except [five] unhappy men who instantly expired.... This melancholy affair was transacted in almost 20 minutes....

Incredibly, in 1767, Townshend came up with a new idea for taxes. The Townshend Acts imposed more taxes on colonial imports—such as paper, paint, glass, and tea—which led to a new boycott throughout the colonies.

Since British soldiers were not well paid, they often worked for local colonial merchants during their off-duty hours. This took away jobs from some of the poorer colonists, which angered them even more.

On March 5, 1770, a group of working men in Boston began taunting and throwing rocks at some of the soldiers. The armed soldiers fired at them, and five people were killed. Colonists referred to the shootings as the Boston Massacre. Captain Thomas Preston, who commanded the British troops, and some of his soldiers were tried for murder, but they were all acquitted. Preston even wrote an account of the bloody incident.

The colonists were very angry that no one was ever punished, but in the end, most of the Townshend Acts were repealed, a move that showed them that they could change British laws by their actions.

THE BOSTON TEA PARTY

In 1773, the British government once again tried to raise revenue by passing the Tea Act. On the night of December 16, members of a rebel group, the Sons of Liberty, decided to stop the tea from entering Boston Harbor and devised an elaborate scheme. George Hewes, a member of the group, provided an account of the evening's "masquerade."

HEWES'S ACCOUNT OF THE BOSTON TEA PARTY: 1773

... I immediately dressed myself in the costume of an Indian ... and ... after having painted my face and hands with coal dust ... I repaired to Griffin's wharf, where the ships lay that contained the tea.... The commander of the division ... ordered me to go to the captain and ... demand of him the keys to the hatches.... I made the demand ... and the captain promptly replied.... We then were ordered ... to take out all the chests of tea and throw them overboard.... In about three hours ... we had ... thrown overboard every tea chest to be found in the ship....

◄ This 1977 poster print is a modern depiction of the Boston Tea Party.

— ★ —

To punish the colonists for their "tea party," Parliament passed a series of laws that enraged the colonists even more. These included the Boston Port Bill; the Massachusetts Government Act; and the Quartering Act, which required colonial citizens to house and feed British troops in their private homes. The colonists referred to the new laws as the "Intolerable Acts."

THE FIRST CONTINENTAL CONGRESS

To respond to these intolerable laws, colonial leaders met in Philadelphia in September 1774 for the First Continental Congress. Among those attending were prominent patriots George Washington, Sam and John Adams, and Patrick Henry. After several weeks of debate, they drafted a Declaration of Rights and Grievances and determined a course of action.

DECLARATION OF RIGHTS AND GRIEVANCES: 1774

... That the inhabitants of the English Colonies in North America, by the immutable laws of nature, the principles of the English constitution, and the several charters or compacts, have the following Rights:

... That they are entitled to life, liberty, & property, and they have never ceded ... a right to dispose of either without their consent.

... That our ancestors, who first settled these colonies, were ... entitled to all the rights, liberties, and immunities of free and natural-born subjects, within the realm of England.

... That the foundation of English liberty, and of all free government, is a right in the people to participate in their legislative council: and as the English colonists are not represented, and ... cannot properly be represented in the British parliament, they are entitled to a free and exclusive power of legislation in their several provincial legislatures....

66 They are entitled to life, liberty, & property, and they have never ceded ... a right to dispose of either without their consent. 99

——— ★ ———

Most delegates hoped for a peaceful resolution, but the British refused their demands, and a boycott of British goods spread all over the colonies. In Massachusetts, the farmers began to form militias. They called themselves "Minutemen," because they would be ready with a minute's warning to fight. In New England, at least, the colonists were preparing for war.

CHAPTER 2

The American Revolution

1775–1787

On the night of April 18, 1775, the governor of Massachusetts, General Thomas Gage, sent several hundred troops to confiscate the weapons of the Minutemen. Three patriots—Paul Revere, William Dawes, and Samuel Prescott—rode out of Boston to warn the colonists.

On April 19, the colonists confronted British soldiers on the town green in Lexington. Shots were fired, leaving eight Americans dead. The British then continued on to Concord, where the colonists had stored their military supplies.

There, the British encountered a much larger force of Americans, and they were forced to retreat. The colonists harassed them all the way back to Boston, killing or wounding almost three hundred British troops in the skirmishes.

With the rebellion quickly spreading, the American Revolution had begun. The next day, British general Hugh Percy reported to Governor Gage on their ordeal.

▲ Paul Revere is riding out of Boston to warn the colonists that the British are coming in this 1953 print.

In obedience to your Excellency's orders I marched yesterday morning at 9 o'clock with the lst brigade and 2 field pieces, in order to cover the retreat of the grenadiers and light infantry in their return from their expedition to Concord. As all the houses were shut up, and there was not the appearance of a single inhabitant, I could get no intelligence concerning them till I had passed Menotomy, when I was informed that the rebels had attacked his Majesty's troops who were retiring, over-powered by number, greatly exhausted and fatigued, and having expanded almost all their ammunition—and at about 2 o'clock I met them retiring from the town of Lexington—I immediately ordered the 2 field pieces to fire at the rebels....

The shot from the cannon had the desired effect, and stopped the rebels for a little time, who immediately dispersed, and endeavored to surround us.... As it began now to grow pretty late and we had 15 miles to retire, and only 36 rounds, I ordered the grenadiers and light infantry to move out first; and covered them with my brigade sending out very strong flanking parties which were absolutely very necessary.... As soon as they saw us began to retire, they pressed very much upon our rear guard, which for that reason, I relieved every now and then.

In this manner we retired for 15 miles under incessant fire all round us, till we arrived at Charlestown, between 7 and 8 in the evening and having expended almost all our ammuni-tion. We had the misfortune of losing a good many men in the retreat, though nothing like the number which from many circumstances I have reason to believe were killed of the rebels. His Majesty's troops ... behaved with their usual intrepidity and spirit nor were they a little exasperated at the cruelty and barbarity of the rebels, who scalped and cut off the ears of some of the wounded men who fell into their hands.

> **"** In this manner we retired for 15 miles under incessant fire all around us, till we arrived at Charles-town.... **"**

THE SECOND CONTINENTAL CONGRESS

The Second Continental Congress met on May 10, 1775. Events in Massachusetts were forcing the delegates to decide between fighting a war of independence and finding a way to settle their disputes with England. In the end, the delegates decided to try a mixture of both approaches.

They asked King George to grant the colonists their rights, but they also began raising money for a Continental Army to be commanded by George Washington. War with Great Britain meant that the colonists were no longer ruled by Parliament and the king. In effect, there was no government. The delegates at the Second Continental Congress decided that its members would serve that purpose. No one wanted war, but the colonists were resolved to die as free men rather than live as slaves.

THE WAR RAGES ON

In Massachusetts, about two thousand British troops were sent to remove the American soldiers, who had taken their positions on Bunker and Breed's Hills, which overlooked Boston Harbor. The Americans tried to hold their ground but were overrun by the British troops, who then regained control of Boston.

The colonists' rebellion spread southward. In June 1775, Lord Dunmore, the royal governor of Virginia, fled to the safety of a British warship in Chesapeake Bay. He promised slaves they would be set free if they fought for the British.

The American planters organized their own army and threatened any slave who ran away with death. In the Carolinas, the colonists also took up arms. At the Battle of Moore's Creek in North Carolina, Americans captured more than eight hundred

▲ A lithograph, c.1897, depicts soldiers of the Continental Army.

British troops. In Charleston, South Carolina, some of the local citizens defeated an attack by British war-ships. There was also military action in Canada, where American forces took Montréal in December 1775 but failed to capture Québec.

Military action was followed by economic actions, as American merchants began to boycott all British goods. Parliament answered with the American Prohibitory Act on December 22, 1775, which not only banned British trade with the colonies but also prohibited trade among the colonies and between the colonies and other nations. At the beginning of 1776, King George decided that he would use Britain's powerful military to crush the rebellion.

THE AMERICAN PROHIBITORY ACT: 1775

... Be it therefore declared and enacted ... that all manner of trade and commerce is and shall be prohibited with the colonies ... and that all ships and vessels of or belonging to the inhabitants of the said colonies, together with their cargoes, apparel, and furniture, and all other ships and vessels whatsoever, together with their cargoes, apparel, and furni-ture, which shall be found trad-ing in any port or place of the said colonies, or going to trade, of coming from trading, in any such port or place, shall become for-feited to his Majesty, as if the same were the ships and effects of open enemies....

◀ This 1909 print depicts a scene from the Battle of Bunker Hill, the first major battle of the Revolutionary War.

VOICES OF THE REVOLUTION

Boycotts and military campaigns were only part of the American Revolution. What people said and wrote were as important, too.

Patrick Henry, a member of the Virginia House of Burgesses, was a leader in every protest against British tyranny and in every movement for colonial rights. He stood before the Virginia Provincial Convention on March 23, 1775, and delivered a stirring speech, encouraging the patriots to take up arms and fight for their freedom.

Patrick Henry is shown delivering his fiery speech in this undated print. ▶

PATRICK HENRY'S SPEECH: 1775

… I have but one lamp by which my feet are guided; and that is the lamp of experience. I know of no way of judging the future but by the past….

Sir, we have done everything that could be done to avert the storm which is now coming on….

Gentlemen may cry, "Peace, Peace!"—but there is no peace. The war is actually begun!… Why stand we here idle!… I know not what course others may take; but as for me, give me liberty, or give death!

Thomas Paine was born in England and raised among farmers and other common people. His formal education was minimal. His first recorded writing was a short article in favor of better salaries and working conditions. Although his mother was a member of the Church of England, his father was a Quaker, and he strongly influenced Paine's views.

Paine had no use for royalty, and he viewed government as a necessary evil. He opposed slavery and was an early supporter of social security, public education, and other ideas that would take a century to achieve.

After meeting Benjamin Franklin in London, Paine emigrated to America in 1774, where he became co-editor of *Pennsylvania Magazine*. He soon became one of the most important voices of the American Revolution. His pro-independence pamphlet, *Common Sense*, was published on January 10, 1776. With more than half a million copies distributed, it was known to every colonist who could read.

Paine encouraged the colonies to fight for independence from tyrannical British rule. He claimed that the discussions about separation from England were based on nothing more than simple facts and common sense.

THOMAS PAINE'S *COMMON SENSE*: 1776

O! ye that love mankind! Ye that dare oppose not only the tyranny but the tyrant, stand forth! Every spot of the old world is overrun with oppression. Freedom hath been hunted round the Globe. Asia and Africa have long expelled her. Europe regards her like a stranger, and England hath given her warning to depart. O! receive the fugitive, and prepare in time an asylum for mankind.

▲ A 1793 engraving of Thomas Paine, the author of *Common Sense*, which was originally published anonymously and became an instant hit in 1776.

THE DECLARATION OF INDEPENDENCE

Paine's words inspired the colonial assemblies as well as their representatives to the Second Continental Congress, who were still meeting in Philadelphia to try to form a national government. They asked Thomas Jefferson, a young Virginia planter, to write a Declaration of Independence.

THE DECLARATION OF INDEPENDENCE: 1776

When in the Course of human Events, it becomes necessary for one People to dissolve the Political Bands which have connected them with another, and to assume among the Powers of the Earth, the separate and equal Station to which the Laws of Nature and of Nature's God entitle them, a decent Respect to the Opinions of Mankind requires that they should declare the causes which impel them to the Separation.

We hold these Truths to be self-evident, that all Men are created equal, that they are endowed by their Creator with certain unalienable Rights, that among these are Life, Liberty, and the Pursuit of Happiness....

We, therefore, the Representatives of the UNITED STATES OF AMERICA, in GENERAL CONGRESS Assembled, appealing to the Supreme Judge of the World for the Rectitude of our Intentions, do, in the Name, and by the Authority of the good People of these Colonies, solemnly Publish and Declare, That these United Colonies are, and by Right ought to be, FREE AND INDEPENDENT STATES; that they are absolved from all Allegiance to the British Crown.... And for the support of this Declaration, with a firm Reliance on the Protection of divine Providence, we mutually pledge to each other our Lives, our Fortunes, and our scared Honor.

◀ This handwritten original of the Declaration of Independence is stored in the National Archives in Washington, D.C. A printed version of it was distributed to the public after it was written.

◄ This painting, c.1794, depicts the signing of the Declaration of Independence. The painting now hangs in the U.S. Capitol.

THE ARTICLES OF CONFEDERATION

After independence from Great Britain was declared in July 1776, the delegates at the Second Continental Congress set out the basic principles and laws of their new country—the United States of America—in the Articles of Confederation. This is considered the nation's first constitution.

ARTICLES OF CONFEDERATION: 1777

Art. I. The [name] of this confederacy shall be "The United States of America."
Art. II. Each state retains its sovereignty, freedom, and independence....
Art. III. The said states hereby ... enter into a firm league of friendship with each other, for their common defense, the security of their Liberties, and their mutual and general welfare....
Art. IV. ... The free inhabitants of ... these states shall have free ingress and regress to and from any other state, and ... enjoy ... all the privileges of trade....
Art. XII. ... And the Articles of this confederation shall be inviolably observed by every state, and the union shall be perpetual....

A TURNING POINT

The war did not go well for the Americans in the early years. When the delegates to the Second Continental Congress issued their declaration, British general William Howe moved a massive military force to Long Island, New York. On August 27, 1776, he attacked Washington and his troops. They were forced to retreat first to Manhattan Island and then to New Jersey. General Howe eventually forced Washington's men across the Delaware River into Pennsylvania.

▲ This print, c.1912, depicts Washington crossing the Delaware River in 1776, in a surprise attack to capture Trenton, New Jersey.

On Christmas night, 1776, Washington recrossed the Delaware, and he and his men defeated some of Britain's hired soldiers from Germany, called Hessians, who were stationed at Trenton, New Jersey. This small victory raised the spirits of the American troops. But when Washington was defeated by the British at Brandywine Creek, he retreated into the hills.

On October 17, 1777, British general John Burgoyne surrendered to the American general Horatio Gates at the Battle of Saratoga, New York. This victory convinced the French that it was time to recognize American independence and join the war on the colonists' side.

George Washington spent the winter of 1777–1778 camped at Valley Forge, Pennsylvania. Under the most difficult conditions, Washington, together with the Prussian officer Baron Friedrich von Steuben and the French Marquis de Lafayette, managed to train the soldiers of the Continental Army, so that they were ready for battle in the spring. In a letter to the Continental Congress, Washington described the terrible conditions his men were enduring and vented his anger at the lack of aid from Congress.

WASHINGTON'S LETTER TO THE CONTINENTAL CONGRESS: 1777

Valley Forge, December 23, 1777

… I am now convinced, beyond a doubt that unless some great and capital change suddenly takes place … this Army [will] … starve, dissolve, or disperse.… [And] … rest assured [that] this is not an exaggerated picture.…

All I can do under these circumstances [is] … to send out a few light Parties to watch and harass the Enemy.… Three or four days bad weather would prove our destruction. What then is to become of the Army this Winter? and if we are as often without Provisions now … what is to become of us in the Spring?…

I have been tender heretofore of giving any opinion, or lodging complaints.… Yet, finding that the inactivity of the Army, whether for want of provisions, Clothes, or other essentials … it is time to speak plain in exculpation of myself; with truth then I can declare that, no Man, in my opinion, ever had his measure more impeded than I have, by every department of the Army.… Soap, Vinegar and other Articles allowed by Congress we see none of nor have [we] seen [them] I believe since the battle of brandywine.… Few men [have] more than one shirt.… A number of Men [are] confined to Hospitals for want of Shoes.…

I can assure those Gentlemen [government officials in Philadelphia] that it is a much easier and less distressing thing to draw remonstrances in a comfortable room by a good fire side than to occupy a cold bleak hill and sleep under frost and Snow without Clothes or Blankets.…

A modern print, c.1944, shows Washington and Marquis de Lafayette at Valley Forge. ▶

THE BATTLE AT YORKTOWN

In the aftermath of the Saratoga disaster, the British decided to attack the South, thinking that because many Southerners were still loyal to the king, they would welcome the British as liberators. By the spring of 1780, the British controlled Georgia and had captured several thousand American troops at Charleston, South Carolina. Then General Lord Cornwallis, the British commander in the South, decided to attack Virginia.

He sailed up Chesapeake Bay and landed at Yorktown, but General Washington and the French were ready for his attack. The Americans surrounded the British on land, and the French navy trapped them by sea.

Lord Cornwallis had no option but to surrender, which he did on October 19, 1781. As General Washington and his officers and men watched, Cornwallis and his almost eight thousand troops laid down their weapons in a huge pile in front of the victorious Americans. Dr. James Thacher, a member of the Continental Army, wrote a vivid account of that British surrender at Yorktown.

THACHER'S ACCOUNT OF THE SURRENDER OF CORNWALLIS: 1781

At about twelve o'clock, the combined army was arranged and drawn up in two lines extending more than a mile in length. The Americans were drawn up in a line on the right side of the road, and the French occupied the left. At the head of the former, the great American commander [Washington], mounted on his noble courser [horse], took his station, attended by his aides....

It was about two o'clock when the captive army advanced through the line formed for their reception. Every eye was prepared to gaze on Lord Cornwallis, the object of peculiar interest and solicitude; but he disappointed our anxious expectations; pretending indisposition, he made General O'Hara his substitute as the leader of his army....

After having grounded their arms and divested themselves of their accouterments, the captive troops were conducted back to Yorktown and guarded by our troops till they could be removed to the place of their destination.

In Great Britain, many people felt that the Americans should have their independence; others simply didn't like the higher war taxes. King George wanted to keep fighting. But Parliament decided to end the war.

In April 1782, members of Parliament met in Paris with representatives from the colonial legislatures. In the Definitive Treaty of Peace of 1783, Great Britain gave up all the land east of the Mississippi River. The United States was now free and independent.

▲ This lithograph, c.1845, is an artist's interpretation of the British surrender at Yorktown.

THE DEFINITIVE TREATY OF PEACE: 1783

His Brittanic Majesty acknowledges the said United States ... to be free sovereign and independent states, and that he treats with them as such ... [and] relinquishes all claims to the government, propriety, and territorial rights of the same and every part thereof.

And that all disputes which might arise in the future on the subject of the boundaries of the said United States may be prevented, it is hereby agreed and declared, that the following are and shall be their boundaries ... from the northwest angle of Nova Scotia ... through Lake Superior ... along the middle of the ... river Mississippi....

SHAYS'S REBELLION

Even with the Articles of Confederation, the national government was weak. There was no president, and there was only one house of Congress. Each state, no matter how big or how small, had one vote.

In order for a law to pass, five of nine delegates had to vote in favor of it. This made passing national taxes almost impossible. Northern states would veto taxes on trade; Southern states would veto taxes on land.

By the time the Revolution was over, the country was broke. It could not even pay the soldiers who had fought for independence. When these troops marched on Philadelphia to collect their back pay, the delegates to the Continental Congress moved from town to town to avoid them.

Times were also hard for ordinary citizens. The taxes that the new states passed made life even more difficult for the poor and the middle class. By 1786, a group of debt-ridden farmers in western Massachusetts, led by Daniel Shays, decided that they had had

JEFFERSON'S LETTER TO MADISON: 1787

Paris, January 30th, 1787

… I am impatient to learn your sentiments on the late troubles in the Eastern states. So far as I have yet seen, they do not appear to threaten serious consequences.…

A little rebellion now and then is a good thing, and as necessary in the political world as storm in the physical. Unsuccessful rebellions … generally establish the encroachments on the rights of the people which have produced them. An observation of this truth should render … republican governors so mild in their punishment of rebellions as not to discourage them too much. It is a medicine necessary for the sound health of government.…

◀ An undated print of Thomas Jefferson, who sympathized with the members of Shays's rebellion.

enough. They took up arms and headed toward Boston. While most government leaders condemned the rebellion, Thomas Jefferson did not and expressed his sentiments in a letter to James Madison.

On the way, Shays and his militia farmers closed down the commonwealth's supreme court in several cities, then turned west to Springfield, where they attacked the federal arsenal to capture the weapons stored there.

Once Shays and his men reached Boston, members of the state government refused to hear their complaints about high taxes, declared the farmers' meetings illegal, and raised an army to fight the insurrection.

Shays and his followers were defeated in a skirmish at Petersham, Massachusetts, in February 1787. Shays escaped to Vermont, but one hundred fifty farmers were captured, and several of them were sentenced to death. George Washington and other national-government leaders urged compassion, and pardons, including one for Shays, were eventually granted.

Shays's rebellion and the issue of taxation made the weakness of the Articles of Confederation even more obvious to the state legislatures. They had loaned money to Congress to pay for the Revolutionary War. If Congress couldn't raise taxes, it couldn't pay back the states.

Great Britain was also demanding the money the United States owed it. Under the terms of the Treaty of Paris, the new American government had agreed to pay all the old debts of the colonies. Without taxes, these bills went unpaid. As a result, the British refused to leave their forts in the West.

To many of the country's political leaders, the rebellion in Massachusetts confirmed what they had believed all along—that the nation needed a much stronger federal government that had authority over taxation and foreign commerce.

A 1787 print of a proclamation signed by Benjamin Franklin offering a reward for Shays and his followers. ▶

PENNSYLVANIA, ff.

By the *President* and the *Supreme Executive* Council of the Commonwealth of *Pennsylvania,*

A PROCLAMATION.

WHEREAS the General Assembly of this Commonwealth, by a law entituled 'An act for co-operating with "the state of Massachusetts bay, agreeable to the articles of "confederation, in the apprehending of the proclaimed rebels "DANIEL SHAYS, LUKE DAY, ADAM WHEELER "and ELI PARSONS," have enacted, "that rewards ad- "ditional to those offered and promised to be paid by the state "of Massachusetts Bay, for the apprehending the aforesaid "rebels, be offered by this state;" WE do hereby offer the following rewards to any person or persons who shall, within the limits of this state, apprehend the rebels aforesaid, and secure them in the gaol of the city and county of Philadelphia ——— viz. For the apprehending of the said Daniel Shays, and securing him as aforesaid, the reward of *One hundred and Fifty* ——— of the state of Massachusetts Bay, an ——— and for th

CHAPTER 3

Forging the New Republic

1787–1789

In 1787, Congress invited delegates, who were wealthy and intelligent men, to meet the following year to rewrite the Articles of Confederation. At the convention in Philadelphia in mid-May 1787, they decided to throw out the Articles altogether and write a new constitution.

The convention considered three major proposals. The Virginia Plan was favored by the larger states and those with claims to land in the West. It called for a strong national government with two legislative houses elected on the basis of population. The New Jersey Plan was favored by the smaller states. It called for equal representation of the states in a single legislative body. The Connecticut Compromise, sometimes called the Great Compromise, broke the deadlock. It proposed a lower house elected in proportion to each state's population and an upper house in which each state, regardless of size, would have equal representation. With this decided, the delegates set about the task of drafting the document.

▲ George Washington addresses the Constitutional Convention in this 1823 engraving.

We, the People of the United States, in Order to form a more perfect Union, establish Justice, ensure domestic Tranquility, provide for the common defense, promote the general Welfare, and secure the Blessings of Liberty to ourselves and our Posterity, do ordain and establish this Constitution for the United States of America.

ARTICLE I. Sect. I. All legislative Powers ... shall be vested in a Congress of the United States, which shall consist of a Senate and House of Representatives....

ARTICLE II. Sect. 1. The executive Power shall be vested in a President of the United States of America. He shall hold his Office during the Term of four Years ... together with the Vice-President, chosen for the same Term....

ARTICLE III. Sect. 1. The judicial Power of the United States shall be vested in one supreme Court, and in such inferior Courts as the Congress may from time to time establish....

ARTICLE IV. Sect. 2. The Citizens of each State shall be entitled to all Privileges and Immunities of Citizens in the several states....

> **Sect. 3.** New States may be admitted by the Congress into this Union....

> **Sect. 4.** The United States shall guarantee, to every State in this Union, a Republican Form of Government....

ARTICLE V. The Congress, whenever two third of both Houses shall deem it necessary, shall propose Amendments to this Constitution....

ARTICLE VI. All Debts ... entered into, before the Adoption of this Constitution, shall be as valid against the United States under this Constitution, as under the Confederation....

ARTICLE VII. The Ratification of the Conventions of Nine States shall be sufficient for the Establishment of this Constitution....

Like the Declaration of Independence, the U.S. Constitution is stored in the National Archives in Washington, D.C. ▶

RATIFICATION OF THE CONSTITUTION

When the convention ended, the thirty-nine remaining delegates (the others had gone home to take care of personal matters) signed the new Constitution. They returned home to try to convince their respective states to ratify the Constitution. A minimum of nine states was needed.

Those delegates who were for ratification were called Federalists because they believed that America needed a strong central government. To educate voters, Alexander Hamilton, James Madison, and John Jay wrote a series of essays known collectively as *The Federalist Papers*, which were published in several New York State newspapers.

Those who were opposed to the Constitution called themselves Anti-Federalists. Most notable among them was Thomas Jefferson. The Anti-Federalists believed that the Constitution had weaknesses that would eventually threaten the freedom that Americans had won. They felt the document as written gave too much power to the national government and not enough to the states.

Like the Federalists, the Anti-Federalists wrote a series of articles that warned of this perceived weakness in the proposed Constitution. They considered themselves staunch proponents of individual liberty and argued that the Constitution should have a "Bill of Rights," the same as many of the states. Their arguments struck a chord with most voters.

New Hampshire became the ninth state to ratify the Constitution on June 21, 1788. A few days later, Virginia and New York narrowly approved it. Because of their size and influence, their ratification was crucial. Rhode Island waited until May 29, 1790.

◀ Articles from *The Federalist Papers* strongly supported adoption of the newly drafted Constitution.

THE
FEDERALIST:
A COLLECTION OF
E S S A Y S,
WRITTEN IN FAVOUR OF THE
NEW CONSTITUTION,
AS AGREED UPON BY THE
FEDERAL CONVENTION,
SEPTEMBER 17, 1787.

IN TWO VOLUMES.
VOL. I.

NEW-YORK;
PRINTED AND SOLD BY JOHN TIEB

▲ This 1940 painting by Howard Chandler Christy depicts a scene at the signing of the Constitution and hangs in the United States Capitol.

FEDERALIST, NO. 1, ALEXANDER HAMILTON: 1787

… After an unequivocal experience of the inefficiency of the subsisting federal government, you are called upon to deliberate on a new Constitution for the United States of America. The subject speaks its own importance; comprehending in its consequences nothing less than the existence of the UNION.…

I propose, in a series of paper, to discuss the following interesting particulars: The Utility of the UNION to your political prosperity. The insufficiency of the present Confederation to preserve that Union. The necessity of a government at least equally energetic with the one proposed, to the attainment of this object. The conformity of the proposed Constitution to the true principles of republican government. Its analogy to your own State constitution—and lastly, the additional security which its adoption will afford the preservation of that species of government, to liberty, and to property.…

THE BILL OF RIGHTS

By the end of June 1788, the Constitution had become law, but some states insisted that there be provisions to protect people from government abuse. Congress appointed a committee under James Madison to consider possible amendments. Twelve were proposed, but only ten were ratified by the states and were called the Bill of Rights. The conflict between the Federalists and Anti-Federalists was finally resolved.

BILL OF RIGHTS: 1791

Amendment I Congress shall make no law respecting an establishment of religion, or prohibiting the free exercise thereof; or abridging the freedom of speech, or of the press; or the right of the people peaceably to assemble, and to petition the Government for a redress of grievances.

Amendment II A well regulated Militia, being necessary to the security of a free State, the right of the people to keep and bear Arms, shall not be infringed.

Amendment III No Soldier shall, in time of peace be quartered in any house, without the consent of the Owner, nor in time of war, but in a manner to be prescribed by law.

Amendment IV The right of the people to be secure in their persons, houses, papers, and effect, against unreasonable searches and seizures, shall not be violated....

Amendment V No person shall be held to answer for a capital ... crime, unless on a presentment or indictment of a Grand Jury, except in cases arising in the land or naval forces, or in the Militia, when in actual service in time of War or public danger; nor shall any person be subject for the same offense to be twice put in jeopardy of life or limb; nor shall be compelled in any criminal case to be a witness against himself, nor be deprived of life, liberty, or property, without due process of law; nor shall private property be taken for public use, without just compensation.

Amendment VI In all criminal prosecutions, the accused shall enjoy the right

to a speedy and public trial, by an impartial jury of the State and district wherein the crime shall have been committed … to be confronted with the witness against him … and to have the Assistance of Counsel for the defense. **Amendment VII** In suits at common law, where the value in controversy shall exceed twenty dollars, the right of trial by jury shall be reserved.…
Amendment VIII Excessive bail shall not be required, nor excessive fines imposed, nor cruel and unusual punishments inflicted.
Amendment IX The enumeration in the Constitution, of certain rights, shall not be construed to deny or disparage others retained by the people.
Amendment X The powers not delegated to the United States by the Constitution, nor prohibited by it to the States, are reserved to the States respectively, or to the people.

▲ A Gilbert Stuart portrait of George Washington, who was the first president of the United States and a member of the Federalist Party.

GEORGE WASHINGTON, THE FIRST PRESIDENT

The men who wrote the Constitution believed it would be almost impossible for the voters to judge properly the qualifications of leaders from distant states. Instead, Congress created the Electoral College, which would be made up of prominent men in each state who knew the candidates.

Each state would have as many electors as it had senators and representatives. The candidate which received a majority of the "electoral" votes would become president. The candidate with the second most votes would become vice president.

In 1789, George Washington was elected as the nation's first president and was sworn into office in April of that year. Congress argued over what to call him. Some suggestions sounded too much like royalty. Finally, everyone agreed on "George Washington, president of the United States."

CHAPTER 4

Conflicts of the New Union

1789–1800

When the French Revolution of 1789 spread to the rest of Europe, Washington proclaimed that the United States was neutral. But despite the country's official neutrality, many American merchants profited by selling military supplies to France. In response, the British blockaded the French coasts and declared that only ships carrying non-military supplies would be allowed to dock.

WASHINGTON'S PROCLAMATION OF NEUTRALITY: 1793

Whereas it appears that a state of war exists between Austria, Prussia, Sardinia, Great Britain, and the United Netherlands, of the one part, and France on the other; and the duty and interest of the United State require, that they ... adopt and pursue a conduct friendly and impartial toward the belligerent Powers;

I have there thought fit ... to declare the disposition of the United States to observe the conduct aforesaid towards those Powers respectfully; and to ... warn the citizens of the United States carefully to avoid all acts and proceedings whatsoever, which may in any manner tend to contravene such disposition.

And I do hereby also make known, that ... the citizens of the United States shall render himself liable to punishment or forfeiture ... by committing, aiding, or abetting hostilities against any of the said Powers, or by carrying to any of them those articles which are deemed contraband.... I have given instructions ... to cause prosecutions ... against all persons, who ... violate the law of nations, with respect to the Powers at war, or any of them....

To circumvent this blockade, American ships began taking military supplies to French colonies in the West Indies, but Great Britain started seizing these ships. Eventually, this stopped, when the British government rescinded its Orders in Council, which had allowed the seizures. President Washington used the opportunity to try to resolve other issues that remained between the two countries. He sent John Jay to London to negotiate a treaty.

Although the British agreed to remove the rest of their troops from America's western frontier, the Anti-Federalists were angry that Jay's treaty contained no assurances that the British would stop attacking American ships. But the Federalists controlled the government, so the treaty was passed.

THE JAY TREATY: 1794

His Britannick Majesty and the United States of America, being desirous by a Treaty of Amity, Commerce and Navigation to terminate their Differences in such a manner, as without reference to the Merits of Their Respective Complaints … may be the best … to produce mutual satisfaction and good understanding….

There shall be firm inviolable and universal Peace….

His Majesty will withdraw all His Troops and Garrison from all Posts and Places within the Boundary Lines assigned by the Treaty of Peace to the United States….

It is agreed that it shall at all Times be free to His Majesty's Subjects, and to the Citizens of the United States, and also to the Indians dwelling on either side of the Said Boundary Line freely to pass and repass by Land, or Inland Navigation, into the respective Territories and Countries of the Two Parties on the Continent of America….

66 There shall be firm inviolable and universal Peace…. **99**

A TREATY WITH NATIVE AMERICANS

While America ceased fighting with the British, colonists still battled with the Indians. In 1794, an American army commanded by Anthony Wayne defeated a Native American force. With this loss, Indians living in Ohio agreed to negotiate a peace treaty. In August 1795, representatives from the various tribes met with Wayne at Fort Greeneville. Together they negotiated a treaty known as the Treaty of Greenville. After it was signed, white settlers began swarming into the Ohio River Valley.

A wood engraving, made between 1850 and 1860, shows Anthony Wayne defeating the Indians in Ohio. ▶

TREATY OF GREENVILLE: 1795

Art. 1: Henceforth all hostilities shall cease; peace is hereby established, and shall be perpetual; and a friendly intercourse shall take place between the said United States and Indian tribes.

Art. 2: All prisoners shall, on both sides, be restored. The Indians, prisoners to the United States, shall be immediately set at liberty. The people of the United States, still remaining prisoners among the Indians, shall be delivered up in ninety days from the date hereof, to the general or commanding officer at Greenville, Fort Wayne, or Fort Defiance....

Art. 3: The general boundary line between the lands of the United States and the lands of the said Indian tribes, shall begin at the mouth of Cayahoga river ... and the said Indian tribes do hereby cede and relinquish forever, all their claims to the lands lying eastwardly and southwardly....

Art. 4: In consideration of the peace now established ... the United States relinquish their claims to all other Indian lands northward of the river Ohio, eastward of the Mississippi, and westward and southward ... [except] the following tracts of land ... one hundred and fifty thousand acres near the rapids

of the river Ohio ... the post of St. Vincennes ... the land ... in possession of the French people and other white settlers ... [and] the post of Fort Massac....
Art. 9: ... The President of the United States ... [shall take] prudent measures ... to preserve the said peace ... until the legislature ... of the United States, shall make other equitable provision ... to the satisfaction of both parties....

POLITICAL DISSENSION

John Adams, a Federalist, won the presidential election of 1796. The Anti-Federalists were now known as "Democratic-Republicans" (today's Democratic Party). Their candidate, Thomas Jefferson, became vice president.

France was angry that John Jay had negotiated a treaty with their enemy, Great Britain, so President Adams sent American diplomats to Paris to improve relations. The French foreign minister refused to meet with them unless they paid him a bribe of $250,000. Insulted, President Adams ended America's alliance with France.

The Democratic-Republicans, who sympathized with France, were branded as foreign agents. In July 1798, the Federalists passed the Alien and Sedition Acts, which were intended to suppress Democratic-Republican dissent. The Democratic-Republicans claimed the acts were an attack on the Bill of Rights.

THE SEDITION ACT: 1798

SECTION 1. Be it enacted ... That if any persons shall unlawfully combine or conspire together, with intent to oppose any measure ... of the government of the United States ... he or they shall be deemed guilty of a high misdemeanor, and ... shall be punished by a fine not exceeding five thousand dollars, and by imprisonment ... [for] not less than six months nor exceeding five years....

SECTION 2. That if any person shall write, print, utter, or publish ... any false ... and malicious writing or writings against the government of the United States ... then such person, being thereof convicted ... shall be punished ... by a fine not exceeding two thousand dollars, and by imprisonment not exceeding two years....

CHAPTER 5

A Government of Wise Men

1800–1815

Thomas Jefferson became president in 1800, but before he took office, President Adams appointed John Marshall, a Federalist, as chief justice of the Supreme Court. Marshall believed in a strong court. In 1803, he used his judicial power and wrote a legal opinion for the case of *Marbury* v. *Madison*, which overturned a law passed by Congress.

John Marshall was the fourth chief justice of the United States Supreme Court. ▶

JOHN MARSHALL'S OPINION IN *MARBURY* V. *MADISON*: 1803

… The question, whether an act, repugnant to the constitution can become the law of the land, is a question deeply interesting to the United States.…

That the people have an original right to establish for their future government such principles as, in their opinion, shall most conduce to their own happiness, is the basis on which the whole American fabric has been erected.…

This original and supreme will organizes the government, and assigns to different departments their respective powers. It may either stop here; or establish certain limits not to be transcended by those departments.

... The powers of the legislature are defined and limited; and that those limits may not be mistaken, or forgotten, the constitution is written....

The Constitution is either a superior, paramount law, unchangeable by ordinary means, or it is on a level with ordinary legislative acts, and, like other acts, is alterable when the legislature shall please to alter it.

If the former part of the alternative be true, then a legislative act contrary to the Constitution is not law: if the latter part be true, then written Constitutions are absurd attempts ... to limit a power in its own nature illimitable.

Certainly all those who have framed written constitutions contemplate them as forming the fundamental and paramount law of the nation, and consequently the theory of every such government must be that an act of the legislature, repugnant to the Constitution, is void.

... If two laws conflict with each other, the courts must decide on the operation of each....

If ... the Constitution is superior to any ordinary act of the legislature; the Constitution, and such ordinary act, must govern the case to which they both apply....

> ❝ If ... the Constitution is superior to any ordinary act of the legislature; the Constitution ... must govern the case to which they both apply.... ❞

Marbury v. Madison was important for a number of reasons. Until this ruling, the Supreme Court had not been considered a very important branch of the federal government. And in fact, Chief Justice John Marshall was only the fourth chief justice to serve in a dozen years.

Marbury v. Madison gave the Supreme Court the authority to declare acts of Congress unconstitutional if they exceeded the powers granted by the Constitution. But even more important, the court became the authority about what the language of the Constitution actually meant. Marshall's opinion made the Supreme Court an equal partner in government—a role it has played ever since.

THE LOUISIANA PURCHASE

In 1803, Jefferson sent diplomats to France to meet with Emperor Napoleon Bonaparte to negotiate the purchase of New Orleans and west Florida. Even though the French still controlled large tracts of land in North America, Napoleon was more interested in finding ways to finance his European wars than he was in keeping his faraway colonies.

The diplomats were surprised that the French government was willing to sell more than 800,000 square miles of Louisiana, between the Mississippi River and the Rocky Mountains. In the Louisiana Purchase Treaty of April 30, 1803, Napoleon agreed to sell the Louisiana Territory for $15,000,000.

THE LEWIS AND CLARK EXPEDITION

Later that year, Jefferson appointed Meriwether Lewis, his personal secretary, and William Clark, an army officer, to head an expedition to explore the Louisiana Territory and the land beyond it to the Pacific Ocean.

Lewis and Clark began their expedition in 1804. They traveled up the Missouri River and across the Continental Divide, which was the western border of the Louisiana Territory, then down the Columbia River to the Pacific. Sacagawea, a Shoshone Indian, helped guide them. Two years later, they returned with maps, journals, and drawings of the new territory.

THE LOUISIANA PURCHASE: 1803

... The French Republic desiring to give to the United States a strong proof of ... friendship doth hereby cede to the United States in the name of the French Republic for ever and in full Sovereignty the said territory [the Colony or Province of Louisiana] with all its rights....

Included [are] the adjacent Islands belonging to Louisiana, all public lots and Squares, vacant lands and all public building, fortifications, barracks and other edifices which are not private property....

The inhabitants of the ceded territory shall be incorporated in the Union of the United States and admitted as soon as possible according to the principles of the federal Constitution to the enjoyment of all these rights, advantages and immunities of citizens of the United States....

▲ An 1810 etching shows Lewis and Clark holding council with one of the many groups of Indians that they met while exploring the new territory.

REPORT TO THOMAS JEFFERSON FROM MERIWETHER LEWIS: 1806

It is with pleasure that I announce to you the safe arrival of my party at 12 o'clock today.... In obedience to your orders we have penetrated the continent of North America to the Pacific Ocean, and ... affirm with confidence that we have discovered the most practicable route ... across the continent by means of the navigable branches of the Missouri and Columbia Rivers....

The Missouri and all its branches from the Cheyenne upwards abound more in beaver and common otter, than any other streams on earth....

Although the Columbia does not ... abound in beaver and otter, ... it ... would furnish a valuable fur trade....

If the government will only aid ... the enterprise of her citizens ... we shall shortly derive the benefits of a most lucrative trade from this source, and that in the course of ten or twelve years a tour across the continent ... will be undertaken ... with as little concern as a voyage across the Atlantic....

> 66 We have discovered the most practicable route ... across the continent.... 99

▲ Sagoyewatha was also known as "Red Jacket" because he often wore a red coat, which he had received from a British officer.

NATIVE AMERICANS HOLD ON TO THEIR WAY OF LIFE

As more and more white settlers pushed boundaries, Indian leaders became alarmed. In 1805 a Boston missionary society asked the leader of the Senecas, Sagoyewatha, for permission to teach their religion to the people of the Iroquois settlements in northern New York State. Sagoyewatha politely denied permission and defended his native religion and his ancestors' way of life when he addressed the Chiefs of the Iroquois Confederacy and the missionary society in 1805.

SAGOYEWATHA'S ADDRESS: 1805

❝ We gave them corn and meat. They gave us poison in return.... ❞

Brother, listen to what we say. There was a time when our forefathers owned this great island.... The [Creator] had made it for the use of Indians. He had created the buffalo, the deer, and other animals for food. He made the bear and the beaver, and their skins served us for clothing.... He had caused the earth to produce corn for bread. All this he had done for his red children because he loved them.... But an evil day came upon us. [The white men] ... landed on this island.... They found friends and not enemies. They told us they had fled from their own country for fear of wicked men, and come here to enjoy their religion.... We took pity on them ... and they sat down amongst us. We gave them corn and meat. They gave us poison in return....

They called us brothers. We believed them.... They wanted more land. They wanted our country.

... Wars took place. Indians were hired to fight against Indians, and many of our people were destroyed....

You have got our country, but are not satisfied. You want to force your religion upon us.... The [Creator] has made us all. But he has made a great difference between his white and red children....

The [Creator]... knows what is best for his children. We are satisfied. Brother! We do not wish to destroy your religion.... We only want to enjoy our own.

AMERICAN TRADE

As president, Jefferson attempted to stay neutral during the Napoleonic Wars between Britain and France. In 1807, the Embargo Act was passed, which forbade all international trade to and from American ports. Jefferson hoped it would keep America out of European wars. But the Embargo Act mostly hurt American merchants.

In 1809, the Embargo Act was superseded by the Non-Intercourse Act, which allowed for the resumption of all trade except that with Britain and France. It was then replaced by Macon's Bill No. 2 in 1810, which allowed trade with Britain and France, but with strict guidelines. Jefferson's experiment with embargoes as a national policy was over.

THE EMBARGO ACT: 1807

... No vessels of any description whatever, and wherever bound ... shall be allowed to depart from any port of the United States without having previously obtained a clearance, nor until the master or commander shall have delivered ... a manifest of the whole cargo on board....

That during the continuance of the act laying an embargo on all ships and vessels in the port and harbors of the United States, no foreign ship or vessel shall go from one port in the United States to another....

THE WAR OF 1812

James Madison was inaugurated as president in 1809, a time of great tension between the United States and Great Britain.

White settlers wanted to take more Indian land in what is now Indiana and Illinois. Indian leaders became alarmed, so Shawnee chief Tecumseh organized a new confederation. He bought weapons from the British army in Canada. In 1811, Tecumseh's warriors fought General William Henry Harrison's troops on the Tippecanoe Creek in Indiana, but they were defeated by the Americans' superior firepower.

Most members of Congress were unhappy with the British for selling weapons to Tecumseh, but when the British began stopping American ships on the high seas, claiming they were looking for British sailors who had deserted, President Madison demanded that they stop. The British refused.

By June 1812, relations between the United States and Great Britain had deteriorated to the point where President Madison decided he had only one option left. He declared war, enumerating familiar grievances: impressment, interference with neutral commerce, and British alliances with the Indians on the western frontier. Madison also saw the war as defending America's independence and honor. Some members of Congress hoped, too, that the United States would conquer and annex British Canada.

Most Americans looked for an easy victory, and at first their troops were successful, but by 1813, the British once again controlled the Atlantic. In 1814, they sailed up the Potomac River to Washington, D.C., and burned down government buildings. Fortunately, Dolley Madison saved many important items from

DECLARATION OF WAR: 1812

Be it enacted by the Senate and House of Representatives of the United States of America in Congress assembled, That war be and the same is hereby declared to exist between the United Kingdom of Great Britain ... and the United States of America ... and that the President of the United States is hereby authorized to use the whole land and naval force of the United States to carry the same into effect....

"THE STAR-SPANGLED BANNER": 1814

Oh, say can you see, by the dawn's early light,
What so proudly we hailed at the twilight's last gleaming?
Whose broad stripes and bright stars, through the perilous fight,
O'er the ramparts we watched, were so gallantly streaming?
And the rockets' red glare, the bombs bursting in air,
Gave proof through the night that our flag was still there.
O say, does that star-spangled banner yet wave
O'er the land of the free and the home of the brave?

the White House before she fled.

After the British burned Washington, D.C., they bombarded Fort McHenry in Baltimore, Maryland. Word soon reached Francis Scott Key, a distinguished young lawyer living in the Georgetown area, that a respected physician of Upper Marlboro, Dr. William Beanes, was being held on a British flagship in Chesapeake Bay. The residents asked Key to help secure the doctor's release.

Key accomplished his mission, but he was detained on the ship overnight during the shelling of the fort. In the morning, he was so delighted to see that the American flag was still flying over the fort that he wrote a poem to commemorate the occasion. It was later set to a melody, and the song eventually became the U.S. national anthem—"The Star-Spangled Banner."

▲ A print, c.1913, depicting Francis Scott Key as he saw the American flag still waving over Fort McHenry in 1814.

THE WAR DIVIDES THE NATION

The War of 1812 divided the United States. Federalist merchants in New England did not support it, because it hurt trade. On December 15, 1814, representatives from five states met secretly in Hartford, Connecticut, to devise a regional strategy to propose new amendments to the Constitution. During the convention, there was even talk of secession.

Although the delegates eventually voted to remain part of the United States, the Hartford Convention angered many Americans. Amid a rising tide of nationalism, they considered what the New Englanders had done almost treasonous. The only thing that came from the convention was that the Federalist Party was never again elected to power.

66 The said States may ... be empowered to assume upon themselves the defense of their territory against the enemy.... **99**

HARTFORD CONVENTION: 1814

[It] is recommended to the Legislatures of the several States represented in this Convention to adopt all such measures as may be necessary ... to protect the citizens of said States from the ... effects of all acts which have been or may be passed by the Congress of the United States....

[It] is hereby recommended to the said Legislatures, to authorize an immediate and earnest application to be made to the Government of the United States, requesting their consent to some arrangement, whereby the said States may, separately or in concert, be empowered to assume upon themselves the defense of their territory against the enemy....

Congress shall not have power to lay any embargo on the ships or vessels of the citizens of the United States, in the ports or harbors thereof, for more than sixty days....

Congress shall not make or declare war, or authorize acts of hostility against any foreign nation, without the concurrence of two-third of both Houses, except such acts of hostility be in defense of ... the United States when actually invaded....

PEACE AT LAST

By the end of 1814, the Americans and the British both wanted peace. In December, diplomats met in Ghent, Belgium, to sign a peace treaty.

Before the news of the treaty reached the United States, there was one more major battle. On January 8, 1815, unaware that the war was over, General Andrew Jackson led his army against a powerful British force at New Orleans and won an overwhelming victory. Until then, the War of 1812 had been an embarrassment for the United States. But the victory in the Battle of New Orleans made Americans feel they had indeed won the war.

PEACE TREATY ENDING THE WAR OF 1812: 1814

… There shall be a firm and universal Peace between His Britannic Majesty and the United States, and between their respective Countries, Territories, Cities, Towns, and People of every degree without exception of places or persons. All hostilities both by sea and land shall cease as soon as this Treaty shall have been ratified…. All territory, places, and possessions whatsoever taken by either party from the other during the war, or which may be taken after the signing of this Treaty … shall be restored without delay and without causing any destruction…. And all Archives, Records, Deed and Papers … shall be forthwith restored….

◀ This 1910 print depicts the Battle of New Orleans. American forces were made up of not only Jackson's army troops but Choctaw Indians, French Creole pirates, and free black soldiers as well.

TIME LINE

1770	▪ The Boston Massacre protests taxation without representation.
1773	▪ The Boston Tea Party protests the Tea Act.
1774	▪ The First Continental Congress meets in Philadelphia.
1775	▪ The American Revolution begins.
1776	▪ The Second Continental Congress adopts the Declaration of Independence.
1777	▪ The Articles of Confederation, the first constitution, is adopted.
1777	▪ General George Washington and his troops spend a cold winter at Valley Forge, Pennsylvania.
1781	▪ British general Charles Cornwallis surrenders to Washington.
1783	▪ The Treaty of Paris officially brings the American Revolutionary War to an end; Great Britain acknowledges American independence.
1787	▪ The Constitutional Convention drafts the United States Constitution.
1789	▪ George Washington is elected the first U.S. president.
1789	▪ The United States Constitution goes into effect on March 4.
1791	▪ The first ten amendments to the U.S. Constitution, known at the Bill of Rights, are ratified.
1796	▪ John Adams is elected the second U.S. president.
1800	▪ Thomas Jefferson is elected the third U.S. president.
1803	▪ The Supreme Court decision of *Marbury* v. *Madison* greatly expands the power of the court.
1803	▪ The United States purchases the Louisiana Territory from France.
1804–1805	▪ Lewis and Clark find a route to the Pacific Ocean.
1808	▪ James Madison is elected the fourth U.S. president.
1812	▪ The War of 1812, fought against Great Britain, begins.
1814	▪ Francis Scott Key writes "The Star Spangled Banner."
1814	▪ The Treaty of Ghent is signed, officially ending the War of 1812.

Glossary

accouterments: equipment other than arms and dress issued to soldiers.

alliances: formal pacts between nations.

avoirdupois: system of weights and measures.

Bill of Rights: first ten amendments to the U.S. Constitution.

blockade: closing off of an area by hostile forces.

boycott: to protest by refusing to buy or use something.

chief justice: presiding judge of a high court.

confederation: group of states united for a common purpose.

embargo: government order prohibiting merchant ships from moving and in out of ports.

Federalist: member of U.S. political party that believed in a strong central government.

Hessians: German soldiers who fought on the side of the British during the American Revolution.

House of Burgesses: a legislative house in colonial Virginia.

impressment: seizure of people or property for service or use.

judicial: pertaining to courts of law.

legal opinion: viewpoint of a lawyer or judge.

legislature: people elected to make the laws for a country.

militia: a citizen army distinct from professional soldiers.

Minutemen: civilians who could be ready to fight within a minute's notice and who fought the British during the American Revolution.

neutrality: policy not to participate in war.

overturned: defeated a law or legal ruling.

Parliament: legislative body of Great Britain.

patriot: person who loves and supports his or her country.

prohibitory: forbidding something.

quartering: act of allowing someone (usually soldiers) to live in a specific house or building.

ratification: act of approving something.

repealed: reversed an act or a law.

republic: government headed by a president elected by the people.

secession: withdrawing from a political union of states.

sedition: behavior or language that incites rebellion against the government.

Supreme Court: the highest court in the United States.

treasonous: betraying one's country.

veto: to reject a proposal or an act.

FURTHER INFORMATION

BOOKS

Fradin, Dennis Brindell. *Signers: The 56 Stories Behind the Declaration of Independence*. Walker & Company, 2002.

Roberts, Cokie. *Founding Mothers: The Women Who Raised Our Nation*. William Morrow, 2004.

Smolinski, Diane, and Henry Smolinski. *Battles of the War of 1812*, Americans at War Series. Heinemann Library, 2003.

WEB SITES

www.historyplace.com/unitedstates/revolution/index.html
An award-winning Web site that presents a six-part chronological history of the American Revolution. There is even a Homework Help section.

www.nps.gov/revwar/about_the_revolution/overview.html This Web site from the National Parks Service of the U.S. Department of the Interior provides a Timeline of Events and Stories on different aspects of the American Revolution, as well as Revolutionary links.

USEFUL ADDRESS

The Smithsonian National Museum of American History
4th Street and Constitution Avenue, N.W.
Washington, D.C.
Telephone: (202) 633-1000

★ ★ ★ INDEX ★ ★ ★